Bodies

Published by:
Powder River Publishing LLC
1014 Black Mountain Road
Thermopolis, Wyoming 82443

Copyright © 2022
ISBN: 978-1-956881-14-1
Printed in the United States of America

Powder River Publishing

www.powderriverpublishing.com

for Nicholas Trandahl

Contents

Part One

Part Two

Part Three

Part Four

Part One

The Doe

Lying in the buffalo grass
along the foundation
of our Wyoming house,
a deer has been dying
for three days.
If we left her there
to disperse like seed
into the cold hard earth
like the rest of us,
she would be eaten alive
by the wind, scavenger birds
or whatever other hungry creatures
roam these streets at night.
It was merciful to call the ranger.
When he pulled up in his green pickup
the deer stood up and sauntered off.
For a moment, I thought
she might turn the corner
and we might watch
her snow-white tail
disappear over the hill.
She collapsed in a heap
before the bullet came.

Horse

The horse holds staunch.
A gaunt, sexless foal.
Its head propped
on the slumped fence.
It trusts. Eating oats
from my outstretched hand.
I fear it will take my fingers
in its square gums and teeth
like the blade of a guillotine.
My aunt has just gone in
for heart surgery. Quadruple
bypass. I wish I could trust
the hand of the surgeon
how the horse trusted mine.

Fences

Slumped fences
skirt this city—
frail, skeletal
like the ribcage
of a weathered oak—
trail markers for snow,
wind and cold.
They are lucky
to be standing,
luckier still
that they have
nothing to hold.

Northern Wyoming

This whole town is a back road.
On our way to the airport, plots
of land surrounded by barbed wire
and chain-link. A few stallions,
foals and mares, old houses,
double-wide trailers, tractor tires,
rusted farm equipment, cemeteries
for a century of pets. An old barn,
its roof caved in as if by a giant fist.
A dilapidated sign swings in the wind,
illegible for years, squealing like a pig.
What was once a wide-open pasture
is now a campground for coal miners.
The day is still young, the sun hiding
behind a field of clouds, as we return
from the airport. I don't know when
I will see my mother again. As we turn
the corner, headed for home, a herd
of pronghorn crosses the road. A lone
buck leads the pack, his curved horns
disappearing over the ridge. This is the
closest I have felt to home since I left
the east coast. I wonder if any of them
will catch him. I wonder if he'll let them.
When our children go down for the night,
maybe we'll make love, maybe we won't.

Mother

She climbs the pine tree
in search of her mother.
Her fingers sticky with sap.

If she doesn't find her
when she reaches the top,
perhaps her mother

will spot her up there.
Perhaps not. I was about her age
when I got lost in the woods

behind my house.
I walked in circles,
the same three birds

soaring over the same trees.
My child brain failed to understand
how every path had grown green

with wild ferns. I cut them down
with a stick and found my way home.
She fell from a broken branch

and broke her elbow.
If she hadn't fallen,
she'd be climbing still.

Using the sticky branches
to build a bridge to the sky.
Searching for the gateless gate

that holds her mother,
in the endless blue reflection
that connects us all.

Falling Water

In the steady orange light
my wife wrings out a cloth,
gently douses him in water.

We keep the fire lit
because of the wind
rattling pipe and vent,
the draft that follows.

Morning light carries
through white blinds,
soft and yellow, like
the wings of a canary.

Doe and fawn graze
under the apple tree
on our front lawn,
bathed in falling rain.

My son, like the fawn,
believes that falling water
is a bath. They both feel it
brushing over their skin,

cleansing their bodies like
a baptism, a rite of passage.

Lonewater Farm

An addiction center for men
was built here in the 1960s.
It was meant to be a place where
men could work the land, fish
and overcome their demons
in the remote Canadian wilderness.
I've never seen it, but I've heard
that its buried deep, somewhere
in the trees. Friends used to tell
stories about mad men running
through these woods. Young men
have wild imaginations, especially
in the country. The center closed
a few years back. Now it's just
a place to fish. An urban legend
in a quaint rural community.
Trout and pickerel gather here,
at this juncture of the Saint John River,
where an aqueduct does its best
to control the water. We watch them
leaping, eager mouths catching air
and blackflies above the surface.
My brother hooks a small fish.
More of a minnow, really. Its gutted,
sputtering on the rocks. Hordes of flies
appear and disappear over the river.
I take a big rock and put the fish
out of its misery. I am only a teenager,
but I am becoming more aware
of my own mortality.

Soul Birds

Yellow light begins
to overwhelm darkness.

A black-capped chickadee
teeters over the wooden cross
near the Sussex Corner exit.

A school bus full of students
from Newton Massachusetts
is fast asleep with their instruments.

The bus flips and rolls down an embankment.

The cross is decorated around the holidays
and the anniversary of the tragedy
to commemorate those who lived and died.

If you stop along the highway
and listen closely
you might hear a chorus of chickadees,
their tender voices rising and falling
over fields of green.

Rabbit

A rabbit stretched

like an elastic band

under an evergreen

hedge. Strung out

across the stern faces

of garden rocks, among

the frost-tipped shrubs.

He must have heard us,

wondering if he was dead.

Like a ghost in reverse,

the rabbit passes from

translucent consciousness

to muscle, skin and bone—

darting across the road,

around the corner

and gone.

Apple

If only I had the wisdom,
poise and beauty of an apple.
The personality of an onion.
The apple hangs like porcelain
below two folded branches.
Skin shining like my wife's legs—
freshly shaven, still wet,
lying open on the bed.
Like Aristotle, the apple asks
for nothing but time.
A simple life of contemplation.
Touch of water, dash of sunlight.

The Lake

for Ben Collins

The lake is not bound to the shore,
the shore is bound to the lake.

—

The sun cuts the lake in half
like a lemon. Your back yard
is a tee box, the gaping lake
a hole that even I can't miss.
White cedar splinters spread
over summer green grass.
My beer and your rum sweat
in mid-August heat. Sometimes,
I feel like the golf ball sinking
to the bottom of the lake.
It must be peaceful down there.
Buried with the eels and amphipods,
sand and decaying plants. The lake
bearing the weight of everything.
An outboard idles in the distance.
Silhouettes cast off to one side.
They fish to stay afloat, we drink.
My heart bleeds like a lemon.

—

The moon is a lemon
slicing through the skylight.

—

Fishing line floats on the lake
like a train of thought.

11

Almost imperceptible, a sliver of silver light
shimmering like memories buried
in the gray folds of my brain.

—

Clouds pass over the lake like busy hands
sifting through the produce section.

—

I've never much liked fishing,
but ever since that hook got lodged
in my right eye, the other in my neck—
I can't seem to separate myself from it.
I feel like I've spent my whole life fishing.
For trout and pickerel. For answers to questions.
For love, meaning and the language to speak it.
Love I've found. For the rest, I'm still fishing.

—

The shore is not bound to the lake,
the lake is bound to the shore.

Bodies

River and Shore

River and shore
are bound to each other
like mother and child.
Strung out along the dock,
cleat knots harness boats
against wind and current.
We loosen the reins
on the neighbor's boat
and glide out onto the water,
your mother's belly round
with your brother.
Tell him this, in case I forget.
Whenever you feel lost,
remember who you are
and where you came from.
Feel the wrinkled knot in your gut.
Know that this is where your body
was tethered to your mother.

Wheelbarrow

A plastic wheelbarrow
glazed with rain water.

Heavy with purpose,
while my son sleeps.

The four silver screws
that hold it together
beginning to rust.

What if we could feel
the rotation of the earth?

There is a moment,
after the rain stops—

after the sun,
the great mortal fire,
has lowered and risen

high enough
to build the earth back up
like a bridge over the water

where I wonder
how many more rotations
these wheels have left.

Imagine listening
to the ceaseless
turning of the earth

its endless motion
the absence
of silence—

turning and turning
like windmills
in an infinite, stable wind.

My son pushes
his plastic wheelbarrow
full of rocks and dirt.

The earth rotates on its axis.

Bodies

Enough

after Ellen Bass

It will never snow enough
to bury mountains. Never rain enough
to fill the Grand Canyon. I don't speak enough.
I think too much. No amount of water is enough
to nourish this desert of yellow grass, bring these roots
back to life, or fill the deep cracks in the chapped earth.
We want & want & want but it's never enough.
We want more time alone, together.
I want your scent to linger longer on my fingers.
Winter lingers like the last apple of autumn.
Summer never stays long enough.

I held back tears as I cut the cord.
The doctor handed you our second son.
His body covered in vernix and blood.
He entered this world face down,
a bulb syringe stuck in his throat.
They call this the golden hour, the hour
of many firsts. Like a fish out of water
he takes his first breath. His gills become
lungs as he takes in your scent. His eyes open,
first encounter with skin and light. First time
feeling a soft nipple harden inside his mouth.
First taste of mother's milk.

Despite all of this beauty and love,
I can't help but wonder if it will be enough.
Will there be enough hours in each day
for you, your brother and your mother?
Will there be enough time left for myself?
Am I enough for my wife and children?

The television flickers in the diminishing
evening light of winter. Body bags cover
the streets of Ukraine. Inside, the bodies
of sisters and brothers, mothers and fathers.
It is suicide to stay in Ukraine, someone told me.
And I suppose they were right, in a way.
Like so many victims of suicide, Ukrainians
who stayed and died had no other choice.

My cousins came home on the school bus
to find their mother hanging from a branch.
She didn't weigh enough to break it.
The rope wasn't weak enough to save her.
The same children found their father
next to a bottle of pills. There wasn't enough time
to wait for an ambulance or pump his stomach.

Sometimes we are given too much,
and this is worse than not having enough.
We are selfish to want & wonder if we are enough.
One of these days I will wake up & appreciate
everything I have, and it will be enough.
I will worship & relish this life like a good meal—
stiff drink, cold beer, good book, passionate fuck.

Part Two

Sparrow

Morning light filters in
heavy on the branch
that holds the sparrow
like an open hand.
Winter tore another hole
in the body of the tree.
The immeasurable weight
of wind and snow
wears on us all,
except the sparrow.
Anyone who is anyone
has flown south by now.
The sparrow nudges ice
and snow aside, shakes off
the cold and takes flight.
The neighborhood cat
lies dead in the road
its eyes like marbles—
lifeless, artificial
like the eyes of a doll.
Lost in a sea of white,
he must have stopped
to rest for a moment,
and died from the cold.
Nothing but frozen fur
under a sheet of snow,
he stares blankly
from his bony sockets
into the crystal abyss
of another cruel winter.
Everything is dead or slow,
even the sky has frozen over.
The sparrow chips loudly,
flitting between a hole
in the snow-covered roof
and the branches above.

Bodies

Patience

I stopped by the fishing lake
along the grassy shoreline
to watch a great blue heron
wait patiently for something
that never came. His legs
were half-submerged, his head
cocked slightly to the left.
Only time could stand so still.
Geese flew over us, the sun
dipped its head behind a cloud
and we stood there with nothing
but wind and water between us—
like strangers in a train station
stopping forever before
passing each other,
the station painted
the bleak grey of winter.
I thought I saw him flinch.
I waited with patience
for him to take flight—
turn his head, take a step,
or stab at the surface for a fish.
When I couldn't wait any longer
I turned away from him
and walked on toward the sun.
I watched its tired light
filter through the trees
and I thought about
how lonely it must be
to be one in a galaxy
of stars, the closest to earth
yet still so far away.
I looked back at the great blue heron
and I imagined his head turning,
watching me walk away
under a cold grey sky,
waiting for me to disappear
from his field of view
like the glimmering scales
of a fish in murky water—
an unknown, nameless star
somewhere in the distance.

Shooting Star

after Ted Kooser's "Meteor Shower"

Just before sunrise,
I look up through
the yawning window
and catch a glimpse
of a shooting star.
A scratch of light,
like a claw against
black construction paper.
It's the kind of scratch
a dog would make
against the window.
An enormous dog
with large enough paws
to leave a smear
on the wide-open
window of the world.

Bodies

Sheep Dog

How lovely the sleeping sheep dog.
Our Slovensky Cuvac, lying in the
back yard. White tufts of fur cover
dead yellow grass like a toupee.
She wakes, startled by some sound
or scent. A cold breeze, perhaps.
Then stands and makes her way
around the yard, her nose pressed
against the earth. When she finds
her spot, she squats on her own pelt,
then flops back down, in a one-hundred-
pound heap. How perfect she would be,
if she could simply learn to love our children.

Flat Spot

The flat spot
on my son's head
is growing as he does.

It's been there since
he passed like a pebble
through the eye of a needle.

The miracle of childbirth.

I used to worry about it,
as if the flat spot might iron out
the rest of his head.

But I have since realized
that nothing, not even the earth
itself, is any more round
than nature will allow.

Dandelions

Dandelions are easier to uproot
than they are to plant.
I remember your license plate
disappearing down the driveway
and out of our lives.
We lived with each parent
half the time. But it was never
the same. One morning
at my aunt and uncle's,
where we lived with you for a while,
I watched the hens mulling about
in their coop. Completely unaware
how delicious they taste roasted.
Their eggs looked like dinosaur eggs,
cartoonish, staring back at me
from the kitchen table.
The difference was in the yolk.
Rich yellow with a touch of white,
instead of the other way around.
Like Mark Rothko's No. 10—
a jubilant, yellow ejaculation
splashed about my breakfast plate.
I remember like it was yesterday,
an elementary school class,
seated in a circle of green grass.
Pulling up milky roots,
watching dandelion fuzz
blowing in the wind
elusive as stars in the night.
One of my teachers told me
that every floating speck was a seed,
bound to become another dandelion.
I found that hard to believe.

Mosquitoes

I held a funeral in my backyard
        for the butterfly I killed
as a child. My mother spoke
        about how everything lives
and dies, and how we should
        always be gentle and kind.
My father taught me not
        to show violence, unless
violence was shown to me.
        I squeezed my swollen skin
beneath a mosquito once,
        to watch the blood rush
fiery and red, like a volcano
        to the surface. Mosquitoes
really do explode, if you
        squeeze hard enough.
The insects exploding against
        our headlights and windshield—
in all likelihood, have lived
        very short lives. I have heard
it said that males live less
        than a week, females no more
than five or six months.
        I didn't hear this, I googled it.
I wonder how the lifespan
        of the mosquito compares
to ours. I am useless at math.
        But I think the difference
is negligible. On the endless
        wheel of time, we both exist
here on earth, for moments.

Moments

Time is a slow burning poison.
It courses through our bodies' red ocean.
There is nothing to be done.
We cannot defeat time, and we
should not defeat ourselves trying.
Nothing is trying to be anything here.
Nothing more or less than a moment
in time. The water of the brook makes
music on the rocks without trying.
Tree branches bend like tall grass
in the wind. The tall grass is home
to flying grasshoppers—all manner
of insect and vermin. Frogspawn
stares back at me from mud puddles
like pupils in black-speckled spume.
The bullfrog croaks and groans
like an old rocking chair. Crickets chirp,
birds sing, mosquitoes whine—
any notion of silence is long forgotten.
The watchful crow caws at the sparrow.
Robins bob for worms in the dew-covered earth.
Somewhere, a child has lost a balloon,
or let it slip from their fingers—it floats
like a tiny moon over a sea of trees.

Leaf

A single green leaf
drifts upon the brook.
It's summer, so the leaves
of the red maple are still green.
The branches above are full
of the same veiny leaves.
How did this one come
to be here, at this time?
I think the odds
of this green leaf
being here, passing me
like a vivid memory
are the same as the odds
of my being born.
This green leaf swims,
triumphant and lonely
as the sperm that swam
the distance, through
the dark moist channel
into existence.

Bodies

Tennis Ball

Lying in the damp grass
its nap peeled back,
folded in on itself
like a cow's tongue.
The pale white rings
on the formerly green
half-eaten tennis ball,
swirl round and round
like the rings of some
strange planet that has yet
to enter our language.
Maybe it is a planet.
Not Pluto either,
or some other planet
we can't decide whether
or not we care about.
But something important.
And as I walk the yard,
picking up fresh thawed
dog shit, I feel glad
for having discovered it.

Body Language

Behind my broken fingernail
is another broken fingernail.
Thin and frail, more sensitive
and transparent. It can't speak,
but it aches and oscillates pain.
I am rubbing my dog's belly
with my foot. It's the only comfort
she needs from me. Besides food
and water, which are also necessities.
We communicate in an ancient dialect.
In the language spoken before music.
The wordless language of beasts and fowls.

Skinning a Deer

"Even when dead, animals want to keep their skin."
— Jim Harrison, "Lazuli Trance"

I watched my neighbor and his daughter
skinning a deer the other day,
with what looked like nothing more
than a pocketknife.
It was sharper, I presume,
because animal skin is tough
even after death, and my pocketknife
can barely break down a box.
Gutted, headless—
its ribcage ripped open,
thick skin peeled back like leather.
I learned, as they hung
the headless deer
from a hook in the garage,
that this process begins
in the field. Its head and antlers
having been removed
as soon as its heart stopped.
It is a Native American tradition
to eat the beating heart
of a fresh kill.
I wonder where they left its heart,
and whether the little knife
they use now to skin it
is the same knife they used
to remove it. I imagine
the beating heart pulsing
on the earthen floor
over a bed of dirt and leaves,
the plump valves and ventricles
a healthy purplish-red,
like my wife's placenta
enveloping the bed pan.

Chainsaw

It was the worst in small spaces:
sharing his bed after a nightmare,
hotel rooms, or in the orphanage—
the title given to the spare bedroom
at my aunt and uncles. He sounded
like a chainsaw cutting wood in the next
bed; a Husqvarna, as my older brother
always said. It startled us from a dead
sleep, we would stir and rise like owls
disrupted in their forest of silence.
It was never the sound that scared us
though, but the silence that followed.
My father's deep-throated, guttural
snoring, followed by what sounded
like choking, then the desperate,
labored breathing, and the longest
silence we had ever heard, repeated,
until the chainsaw started up again.

Bodies

The Middle of the Night

Bright light is unbearable
in the middle of the night.
We shrug it off, turn and hide
our eyes like indifferent shoulders.
The world only makes sense
in the middle of the night
in small doses. We understand
from experience and instinct
how to find the things we need
the way a breast-fed baby
finds its mother's nipple
without the ability to see.
The middle of the night
is a transitional phase —
a stage between wakefulness
and sleep, a plane of existence
between the dead and the living.
You can see cartoons flashing
on the pitch-black television screen
in the middle of the night.
You can remember all the words
to *Good Night Moon.* You can remember
the moon waning, its white light fading
like decaying teeth. But your middle name,
where you work and what you do
never enters the equation. These details
never trigger, never reach the synapses
in the enigma that is your brain.
The darkest hours are the longest
in the middle of the night.
Sinking into the living room couch,
when the stars don't shine
and the cosmos is an endlessly vast,
wasteland of empty darkness.
The god of darkness lives here
in the middle of the night
and he never rests,

only existing in absence.
No human being is awake
at this hour. Except
the coal miner returning
from his night shift. The lights
of his lifted truck like sunbeams
announcing the arrival of morning.
The coffee pot is switched on,
a lighter shade of darkness sets in,
a flock of geese honks overhead
and begins to make its descent
over the house, upon the lake.
This is all the confirmation I need
that the middle of the night has ended,
that morning will come
and another day begin.

Fog

The day unfolds like a body
       half-awake
             under a blanket
of fog. Heavy folds of light
       billowing from
             the streetlamp,
opaque as a trauma-buried
       memory. Last night
             I dreamt my wife
and children died in a car accident.
       The air was thick
             with fog, yellow lines
and stop signs invisible
       outside the windows.
             This morning, they sleep—
my wife next to me, youngest
       on the monitor, snoring softly
             as his white noise machine,
eldest wedged between us
       like a body pillow. We all
             woke up this morning,
but a piece of me still exists
       in the alternate reality
             of that dream—hungover,
half-drunk, passing through life
       like dim headlights piercing
             the weight of fog-dense air.

Anxiety

The harbor is a flat rock,
the ocean cloaked in fog.
I stand alone on the dock,
drinking coffee, watching
tugboats skim the surface,
disappear on the horizon.
I wonder who knows I am here.
I wonder who cares.
I can almost hear the Reversing Falls—
Saint John River and Bay of Fundy
converging in the gorge,
white-water whirlpools whipping.
A wharf rat emerges
as if from under a rock.
I sweep the cold gray floor
of the shop, the air still wet
with fog, thick and heavy
as the fat brown rat.
It stares at me for a while,
as if preparing to speak.
Its black eyes like bowling balls,
my skinny white body the last pin.
When the fog lifts, hours later,
I think of the wharf rat disappearing,
its claws dragging like knuckles
against the earth, as it burrows
back into the deep dark channel
from which it came.

My Wife

after Raymond Carver

My wife appears fully clothed
at the top of the stairs.
She has come up from work
to pump the bulge of milk
from her left breast.
When she descended them
this morning, I loathed myself
for wanting to take in
her mammalian scent—
staring at her panties
lying open on the carpet
at the foot of the bed.

Bodies

for Jacqlyn

Red clippers and a pair of scissors
from the butcher's block.

A modest blend of brown and gray
collected in tufts on the tile,

clung to plastic bristles.
The steady buzz weakens

my already heavy eyelids.
Maybe it's the stiff drink,

or your fingers parting my hair
that has me feeling sentimental.

Maybe it's your tender breasts, braless,
in one of my shrunken t-shirts,

your nipples brushing like knuckles
over my shoulder blades.

I am blessed by your touch.
When I feel your weight and length,

the pressure of your body laid over mine,
I feel the weight of everything.

Like the earth bearing the weight
of time, I am fully aware.

I run my fingers through your hair,
over the lotus that blossoms

from the notches on your spine.
And I have never felt more alive.

Bodies

But I can't stop thinking
that one of us is going to die

first. I can hardly bear the thought.
Skin and bone, bone and skin.

This is how we have evolved.
Perhaps we have come too far.

Take me back. Or bury me here,
beneath the soft walls of your body,

under the weight and length that binds us.

Part Three

Spring

My tea is turning cold.
      The tea bag drips
            like melting snow.

Spring has disappeared
      faster than the clock
            sprung forward.

Snow clings to the earth
      like cellophane to a white
            paper plate. I've been trying

to get that hour back, but
      I can't move fast enough.
            Winter has a mind of its own.

Yesterday, a robin landed
      on our grey deck erased
            by a mountain of snow.

It seems the birds had it wrong.
      The neighbor climbs a ladder
            searching the rain gutters

for a leak above his garage.
      To get back the time I lost,
            I'll have to wait until fall.

The Bearded Woman, by Ribera

"Such a handsome boy you were,"
my aunt tells me while flipping through
the pages of an old photo album, her eyes
and brain ticking like the arms of an old clock.
The evening air burning with fireflies.

> She sees herself in each
> faded photograph.

Earlier versions of herself.
The bodies they occupied back then.
The healthy bodies with healthy beating hearts.
Long before the quadruple bypass.

> The fireflies disappear
> in the cloud cover.

She pours another drink,
moves to the gazebo and lights a cigarette.
A veil of mist drapes the evening air.
She turns the page. Stopping at a photograph
of her daughter in front of the bathroom mirror
with Q-tips in her ears.

> She braces herself for the
> memory flooding back.

Her daughter swallows painful sobs.
Blood trickles from her ruptured ear drums.
My aunt's brain wanders from this bloody scene,
to the day her daughter became a woman.
I imagine the moment as a ceremony.

> A red rose emerging
> from a lotus blossom.

Spring transforms everything.
The world is beautiful in transition.
Lakes and rivers no longer frozen,
the water free to breath in the open air.

A recent photograph
somehow snuck in there.

My beak is pulled down, angular,
shading my large nose. My glasses
snug as a bandage over its bridge.
My beard red as the evening sun.

Now her daughters
dress me in their clothes.

My curly brown hair in pigtails.
A red dress, heavy blush, a pair of quiet heels.
These two photographs converge like clouds in my head.

The bearded man &
the boy dressed as a girl.

Heels click softly against the laminate.
My voice changes from tenor to baritone.
Now Ribera's painting, The Bearded Woman.
A foreboding image to say the least—

urging the displaced viewer
to stare & avert their gaze.

Or is it Ribera? The severe tone of the piece
captured in stark colors and solemn faces.
The background overshadowing
the forlorn expression of Magdalena's husband

who appears less man,
and, invariably, less woman,

than his wife. Masculine figure and jawline.
Vacant eyes & plain clothes, delicately
stitched by the stroke of a brush.

Magdalena's long beard
& plump, cyclopic breast.

What is it about myself as a bearded man,
and a young boy dressed as a girl,
that has me so utterly transfixed?

I look in the mirror at the
born boy and become man.

Flowers

The other day, my wife asked me
to never buy flowers for her again.
They are beautiful, but I can't stand
watching them die on the kitchen table.
Not to mention, flowers aren't worth
the price, and I am sick of collecting vases.
Flowers wilt like time-compressed bones.
Roses begin their descent after Valentine's Day,
carnations & hydrangeas after Mother's Day,
poinsettias dying a much slower death
on the days leading up to & after Christmas.
From the day we are born we begin dying.
But the death of a flower is necessary,
natural and beautiful as its emergence.
Next time I will pick wildflowers
from the side of the road
and bring them home to her.
Or, better yet, perhaps I should replace
the artificial flowers on our kitchen table.
Even the undying needs replaced,
its lifeless color drenched in sunlight.

Peacock

At first, I thought they were mountains.
       Staring up at their tilted beaks.
Their necks craning, heads adorned
       with bushy green trees. Then,
I noticed green-blue feathers, hundreds
       of turquoise eyes beneath
a cold grey sky—staring back at me
       with the judgment of saints
painted on stained glass. The peacock
       doesn't understand its own beauty.
The saints don't judge us. We judge ourselves
       because of the saints. My wife keeps
staring at herself in the mirror, trying
       to see herself through my eyes.

Doors

Before the golf course, at the old border
between Grand Bay and Westfield,
there is an archway of trees. A network
of branches and leaves delicately woven
like the doilies my grandmother used to weave.
The magnitude of its beauty makes me tremble
whenever I enter it. The moon spills through
our bedroom window like a ring light, illuminating
the notches of your spine. Whenever I think
of the doilies on my grandmother's kitchen table,
I think of the lotus tattoo on my wife's back,
the ink woven into her skin like a spider's silk.
The spiderweb is the key to the spider's survival.
The lotus marks the border between air and water.
My wife holds the key to the doors of our future.

Tremble

The sun has all but disappeared.
Its last light shines behind
the mountains. How exhausted
it must be, rising and falling
like the tide. We rise over
and over with our children
while the sun and tide sleep.
A constellation of cars and trucks
spread across their ceiling from
the box of light on the floor.
The streetlamp creeps between
the gaps in our blinds.
Our bodies dance in shadows
like hands on the white walls.
I run my fingers over the lotus
spread across your back
like a pair of wings.
Our bodies were built for each other,
sculpted by passion and experience.
Overcome with emotion,
I tremble over your skin.
The very same way I trembled
when I watched you crowning.
Nothing could ever prepare me for this.
You arch your back, rise to your knees
and roll over onto your side.
For the rest of my life,
as sure as the sun and the tide
I will tremble every time.

Becoming Mountain

after Shangyang Fang's "Argument of Situations"

The bearded man walks in the mountains.
Sunlight follows him
embroidered with branches
and mountain shadows.
Rivers lakes streams rocks trees.
Shape among shapes, color among colors.
Consciousness walking.
Rivers lakes streams rocks trees.
Bull moose and bison watch him pass
like wind through the trees, sediment
blowing in the mountain breeze.
Rivers lakes streams rocks trees.
This man is a brushstroke, a breath
of alpine air, a streakline on the mountainside.
Rivers lakes streams rocks trees.
Boots and journal his essential companions.
Orange flannel visible through the trees
like a hunter's vest. But he is no hunter,
unless mountains can be hunted.
Rivers lakes streams rocks trees.
Come winter, he will be walking still.
His red beard whitened with frost.
The mountain man is never lost.
Rivers lakes streams rocks trees.
He desires nothing but walking and writing.
Nothing is too difficult to desire.
Rivers lakes streams rocks trees.
He has buried himself in the mountains.
Traded in bones and skin
for rock, tree and plant.
Rivers lakes streams rocks trees.
It must get lonely up there. He must be scared.
But the mountain is never lonely.
The mountain is never scared.
Rivers lakes streams rocks trees.
He marches up the mountain.
His feet striking the earth like percussion instruments.
The music in his head a string quartet.
Rivers lakes streams rocks trees.
When he reaches the summit he will pitch a tent,
descend the mountain and climb it again.

47

The Pastor Takes a Walk

after Frank McGuinness

The pastor goes for a walk along the beach.
Beneath a cloudy sky, a shoreline of bare trees.
Listening to the crescendo of the Coral Sea.
Somewhere, an astronomer and a physicist
scour the cosmos with a fine-tooth comb
like a mother searching her child's hair for lice.
Elon Musk contemplates human extinction,
the inevitable end of life on earth.
Meanwhile, a paleontologist studies the ivory
tusks of a woolly mammoth. Another cleans
and polishes dinosaur bones and teeth.
Something washes up along the beach,
a corpse swollen with saltwater and heat.
On another planet, a washed-up cadaver
would raise even more suspicion.
Human hands, lizard tail, Neanderthal skull.
Professors argue that the pastor's alien
is nothing more than a swollen possum,
washed into the ocean in a recent flood.
But now the pastor questions everything.
When he delivers his sermons, he thinks
about the alien washed up on the beach.
He questions his faith, the age of the earth,
Christ's birth, death and resurrection.
The sanctity of organized religion.
He questions the observable, finite universe.
The quality of air and water he consumes.
He doesn't consider himself a pious man,
but he has given so much to the church.
Lately, he finds himself praying to the stars.
Listening to the crescendo of the Coral Sea.
Beneath a cloudy sky, a shoreline of bare trees.
The pastor goes for a walk along the beach.

Bodies

Burial

Grapefruit skies turn blood orange.
My dog whines and paws the earth
around a tiny, featherless bird.
Its skin like the skin of raw chicken,
premature wings and swollen lips splayed
in the shadow of the live oak.
Kildeer shriek, wings walloping
toward the rising sun. The moon
buries itself in the mountains.

Mountains

I'm headed to the mailbox
to pick up toothbrushes,
rapid tests, and my copy
of Burying the Mountain.
Our house is a mountain,
to the layer of fallen snow.
The layer of snow is a mountain,
to the earth buried below.
My breath is white and floating
like a cloud. Some chemical compound
lighter than air. It rolls away like steam
over the lake. The sun has reached its peak—
a yellow mountain covering the earth
with her blanket of warm light.

The River

Wild horses graze in the breeze.
The river beckons and brays
in the direction of your burial place.
Even though I carry your words
in my head like a maze, I imagine
you buried at the base of a mountain.
The river bends its neck through the trees.
The earth coils around you like granular snakes.
Branches above cross and curl
like pubic hair, naked legs.
Birds from Mexico fly low over your grave,
headed north. Only your wife, daughters
and closest friends know you are here.
The rest are left to wonder.
There is magic in this privacy and loneliness.
Wonder is where magic begins.
Are you really dead? Or simply hiding
from the world, living like a monk.
Poetry your scripture, your words
the definitive music of the afterlife.
No coffin or hole in the ground
can hold your past or future.
You are buried only in the present.
Wild horses graze in the breeze.
The river beckons and brays
in the direction of your burial place.

Dead Deer

Scattered bones
curled like ivory tusks
in the wooded green.
Gnarled antlers—
crown of thorns
above naked skull.
A hairline fracture
below barren ribcage
like the scar
of an appendectomy.
Skin and sinew flayed
by a pack of coyotes—
exposed bones picked clean
by maggots and scavenger birds.
Ice and snow preserved
this frail skeleton.
Now dandelions, tangled weeds,
peat moss and wild ferns grow
around scattered bones.

Small Birds

*"Birds make mistakes, so many dying
against windows and phone wires."*
—Jim Harrison, "The Golden Window"

Watching them glide like sprites
on the forgiving August air,
it's hard to imagine anything
less than perfection.
But birds make mistakes,
just like us. We are alike
in more ways than one.
As a boy I heard a beak
crash like a stone against
our neighbour's window.
I imagined its limp body
in the flower bed—
skinny bones and
weightless feathers
in Diane's fingers.
I've never seen a bird of prey
lying like deer or vermin
along the interstate.
What do they know
that the small birds don't?

Goshawk

The northern goshawk
lives on the light post
out on the main road.
A mix of pale and slate-grey,
standing tall and sleek
as a bachelor's robe.
The field across the way
is busy with pronghorns
grazing on sagebrush.
As if from a dead sleep
the goshawk falls from its perch,
arches its wings and drops
like a scythe into the ditch.
The tail of a mouse or mole
slithers from its beak
like the tongue of a snake.
I catch a glimpse
of one gleaming orange eye
as the goshawk tilts back its head
and swallows it whole.

November

Its sixty degrees
in the last week of November.
A bee buzzes nonchalantly around my head.
The fishing lake has frozen over,
all the geese have flown away
to some distant corner of the world.
Or the field across the street.

Skilsaw

The Monday afternoon geese
honk like foreign cars
searching for a parking space
as they fly in from out of nowhere
over the frozen fishing lake.
Yesterday children shoveled off space
to play and skate, tomorrow
the sun might get warm enough
to melt a landing strip
of frigid water for the geese.
If I had their wings
I would pack my family in suitcases
and head south for the winter.
But I'm only human.
And I have read the myth of Icarus.
The only sound I have heard
since the echoes of their honking
tapered off, becoming music
to the wind, is the crunch
of snow beneath our feet.
Houses are visible now on the horizon,
signs of civilization that seem
to approach us as we approach them.
If I listen close enough
over my loud-footed dog
in this dead winter silence
I can hear a skilsaw
sounding off in the distance
like a carpenter's impression
of a skilsaw.

Bodies

Casper

Horse heads dip,
pitman arms bend,
mechanical elbows
swing in the wind.
A family of mule deer
stands motionless
in dead yellow grass.
Icicles hang like daggers
from the passing road signs.
Horses and cows stand frozen
under the winter sun.
Dirt roads in the distant
hills of pine, and a sign
that reads: Carbon Creek.
Snow-covered mountains
cast monumental shadows
over the city of Casper.

Snowmobile

His body was a block of ice
when they found him.
His head on the other side
of the barbed wire property line.
His snowmobile still running,
breathing a little warmth
into the cold night.

Incense

with an opening line by Dan Gerber

Tonight the sky is holding its breath.
Clouds of fog spattered under the trees,
over white vinyl fences. Geese glide in silence
over a glass lake. The wind runs its fingers
through the trees. It whispers to the lake,
sending shivers down its spine. The dog
is curled like smoke in the grass. The sound
of thunder closes in: flash of lightning,
flurry of hail. The wind takes the grill
by the handle and flips it off the deck.
A wisp of charcoal escapes from the vents,
disappearing like incense over the fence.
My grandmother has been dead five years.
She was cremated. At her funeral, the priest
burned incense and flicked holy water at her casket.
Could this be her, flying on the wind?
So much depends upon belief and religion.
We are all specks of dust, in the end.

Death

"Let's not get romantic or dismal about death.
Indeed it's our most unique act along with birth."
—Jim Harrison, "Death Again"

Someone told me that even after we die,
our hair and fingernails continue to grow.
But this is a myth. I used to imagine hair
sprouting through skull and pubic bone.
Fingernails growing like roots. But follicles
can't exist without skin. And dead bones
are just dead bones. Without muscle
and tissue, organs and blood pumping
through them, we cannot live. Our bodies
are lifeless as sailboats without sails,
stripped bare and buried. In the end,
our bones are just bones without bodies,
our bodies just bodies without souls.

March

It's nearly sixty degrees again
and the birds have already returned
from however far south they managed
to fly. Snow is in the forecast for the weekend.
But I trust the birds more than the weather network.
We are skeptical about the groundhog, but we trust birds
flying over us like small gods. Watching over us like
small gods. Trying not to intervene until called upon.
I am walking with my sons. One is fast asleep.
The other kicks a clump of grass along the sidewalk.
A spider clings to the stroller cover. Eight tiny legs
methodically sprawled. He is so small
he looks like he was just birthed. I call him he
because it hurts less if I have to kill him.
When I was a boy, a pregnant spider birthed
a million babies under the weight of my finger.
I take the same finger that killed the spider-mother
and flick him into oblivion. Birds chirp, diving
between branches, rooftops and powerlines.

Harrison

Where was I when Jim Harrison died?
Trying my hand at poetry? Half-drunk
wandering the streets of Dublin?
I never read a single Harrison poem
while he was alive. I imagine his death
face down on his writing desk.
His right hand clutches a pen, left
reaches for his last glass of whiskey
or red wine. A potted plant sheds a leaf
in the corner of the room. The leaf grows
into a spiral of trees. Their roots and limbs
coiled like rattlesnakes, breaking through roof
and ceiling, letting in thousands of birds.
Cardinals, robins, sparrows, sandhill cranes
and a single great blue heron. All manner
of winged creatures—some whose names
I can't remember, some I've never seen.
They have come to give you your wings.
Not to take you to heaven. That place
doesn't exist. Not for men like you,
at least. They are taking you to the river.
Returning you to the water where all life
begins and ends. The endless river where
gods and the poets who revive them live.

New World

Pockets of dense clouds cast shadows
over the lower half of the distant mountains
and the wind sundered, flat topped, cantaloupe hills.
Closer to I-90—dry rot stumps, buffalo grass,
tumbleweeds, and a lone standing tree—
the other ripped up at the roots. A wooden cross
large enough to hold the body of Christ,
leaning like a weather worn fence post.
Brown cows lift their skull-white heads in unison.
Pronghorn graze in the dead valley.
Spearfish creek feeds into the fish hatchery.
The bare bones of an old fishing boat,
a museum, and a train car—memories dug up
and placed here like skeletons. Rainbow
and brown trout whipping torso and tail
below the surface, their slender mouths
hungry for vending machine pellets.
I watch the two who couldn't be bothered
by the commotion. One is swollen with eggs,
the other is blind—his kype unhinged,
milk-blue eyes jogging in their sockets.
The stroller is hunched in the shade
of a swaying pine. A rainbow trout floats
on its spine. A hundred flies sunbath
on an informative sign: Warning, Poison Ivy.
Silver-flecked spawn huddle in a shallow pond.
A pair of geese are teaching something
to their fluffly yellow offspring
on a deserted island. A green-headed mallard
bobs for small fish, its orange feet
and feathered rump flailing in desperation.
A pair of inukshuks rest on the cliff peak.
A little girl, half-naked, dips her toes
in the shallow stream. An Asian boy
with a mask strapped to his face.
Scaly grey trees, skin peeling like scalps—
the cliff face covered in sunburnt sagebrush.
A single grey cloud spread across the sky.
This new world is buried in grey light.
Lifeless, concrete dust, like the aftermath
of a collapsed building, the scattered ruins
of some ancient civilization. Until the sun
descends like a staircase down the mountain,
and the world is made colorful again.

Part Four

I Remember the Vultures

after Ada Limón

Seagulls litter the sky over the hospital
squawking and squawking as the crow caws
from the highest branch in a row of trees.
The robin pecks at the dew dampened soil.
I remember my wife telling me about the vultures,
eagles of the city, flooding her San Antonio office.
Black silhouettes cast against the clear blue sky,
crooked talons hooked into hot concrete,
brooding eyes wandering from the precipice,
bald red heads shining like the scar that's left
after a loved one's death.

San Antonio

Dust particles and skin cells float
on a warm shaft of light.
Yesterday it was spring.
Today it's winter again.
Sometimes the sun is so warm
this cold becomes bearable.
I take out the trash shirtless,
barefoot. Sometimes I go back
to San Antonio. I sit in a chair
on the concrete slab we called our deck,
crack a Corona or Busch Light
and listen to steaks sizzle on the
charcoal grill, the honeybees humming
like a refrigerator on its last legs.
My father sits on a lawn chair
in the grass, drinking a caesar.
We don't speak. We just listen,
drink, and wait. My wife is here
somewhere, but our kids aren't.
After we eat, my father leaves.
She comes out dressed in a bikini.
She doesn't know how sexy she is.
She wears it because it's hot, because
she can, and because she likes to please me.
She knows I like it. Her plump breasts and thighs
are covered in tiny sweat beads. Her figure
reassures me that our children are alive.
Butterflies flutter over the canopy,
swimming in the warm light like minnows
in a shallow brook. Back in Wyoming,
it's twenty degrees and snowing.
In moments like these I would rather
be the butterfly or the minnow.
But my wife and children wait for me
inside. And it can't be easy
to constantly swim or fly.

Trying on Tuxedos

for Justin and Shelby

Today I'm thinking about the afternoon we spent
trying on tuxedos for your wedding.

The memory comes to me like the fresh scent
of New Mexico Piñon Coffee —

the wrinkled hands of a man who has only known
the gentle labor of retail

measuring our arms and legs,
necks, waists and inseams

lifting the inserts from every shade
and style of brown dress shoe

pulling jackets and pants from their hangers,
folding them with the ease and care of a tailor.

I look down now, at my diaper soiled hands,
cobalt chrome shining on my third finger

from the sunlight that seems, just now,
to have entered the kitchen.

It seems I knew nothing then.
My hands and mouth had yet to feel

a woman surrender herself completely —
scratch, claw and moan like a bear

tilling fertile soil, the fruits of my labor
spilling like loam from her powerful jaws.

I never knew this kind of love.
The raw and tender meat

of the days and years to come.
I never knew the love of fatherhood,

despite having felt it from my father.
I never knew the bond that comes

from watching a goddess on earth
bear and raise your children.

I never knew any of this. But as I stood
under the arches, in the green grass

of your bride's backyard, watching you
watch your fiancé walk down the aisle,

I caught a glimpse of it.

Discovery

I'm sitting down
with Jim Harrison
again. His words
illuminate this room
more than the lamp.
This is the time of night
that I can sit in dim light
and discover myself.
The beer and the whiskey
are starting to hit me.
The white wine was barely
traceable on your lips.
Tonight, I discovered
that your scent
makes me quiver
like a bee on a flower.
I already knew this,
but I discovered it again.
The gods are half-drunk,
but they speak to me
about a warm river
that flows like milk
through the cavernous
mountains. The evening
is silent. I slide into bed
on my back and roll over—
I'm all in. I'm all yours.

Jamaica

There's something about swimming at a beach
in water deep and dark enough
that I lose sight of what's beneath
that sets my teeth on edge.
After the shuttle driver sold us a bag of weed
somewhere between the resort and the airport,
I couldn't stop seeing the cannabis green leaves
on the tops of the palm trees.
We smoked and smoked and smoked
until the scent of the green plant
clung to our fingertips like sex.
Sitting on the balcony in the predawn
darkness, smoking weed and hash,
the glare of the streetlamps fading
like smoke rings, I pretended to believe
in God. Not because I feared death,
even though I do. Not for any other reason
than to have someone to speak to in my head.
I told myself that my body was an ocean,
treading water under my sun-bleached skin,
and I prayed to my newfound God
that I might find the strength
to brave the inlet's deep blue.
Morning came, and I forgot all about
my Jamaican God. I dipped my toes
into the ocean, then returned to the pool.

Bodies

Human

Gods were everywhere
when I was a boy.
They were in the woodsmoke
of a summer breeze.
They were in snowflakes,
the throbbing veins of leaves,
mud thawing beneath our feet.
They were in dragonflies
getting their rocks off
mid-flight. They were in bees
touching down on the dandelions
of our overgrown lawns.
Silence gave them their voice,
all I had to do was listen.
Now they are few and far between.
I used to hear them down by the river
skimming across the water
like flat rocks. One spring
the ice melted so fast
that the bridge flooded.
A man named Beaver
tried to drive his truck through it.
He disappeared near the middle,
climbed out the rolled down window
and onto the roof. The water
was ankle-deep, his truck sunk
like a ship at sea. He stood there
hovering over the water
and yelling into the wind
like an angry god.
It was colder, certainly—
when I was a child.
And there was more snow.
School was cancelled constantly.
Did the gods of my youth perish
in that flood? Did they move
somewhere colder? Or was it
my aging that killed them?
Perhaps children are small gods
and as we grow older,
we become human.

Last Night

This morning is a morning like any other,
but last night was different.
You rise and flop your breast
into Rowan's mouth.
His thin lips sip your milk
like a hummingbird pulling nectar
from a budding sunflower.
You float past us in a baggy t-shirt
and parachute pants, glass of water in hand,
as we listen to the drip-drop suck
of soaked coffee grinds
emptying themselves into the pursed lips
of the pot. Last night we redefined the term
animalistic. I could have crawled all over
the walls of this house, my six-legged body
buzzing like a fly searching for light,
every fibre of hair on my body lifting
straight into the air like the hair of a fly,
my eyes watching you, magnified,
all 360 degrees of you. I could have flown,
clung to your sweat like dragonflies
in the heat of summer. I buried my face
in the vortex of your braids,
let them wrap me up and suck me in
like tentacles. Last night, our bodies were mountains.
We fingered and muscled our way to their peaks.
I want to go back there, to that place
where the laws of time and space
are suspended. Where five minutes
is an hour, and an hour is five minutes.
I want it all over again. I don't want it to end.
But would I still appreciate it?
Would I still worship
the dimples on your lower back and lip,
the delicate, wing-like, angular corners
of your eyelids, the tender hairlessness
of the back of your knees?
You are sipping coffee, thumbing groceries
into the app on your phone, the early light
shining over last night's thin layer of makeup,
nibbling your lip in concentration,
trying to focus on a thousand things
instead of one, like last night,
when we both shined, to each other,

like the last star on earth.

Bodies

The Frog

after Ada Limón's "Overpass"

These roads were bare back then,
nothing but chipseal and hockey nets.

The afternoon air hummed a bass chorus.
Evenings, a symphony of flickering amber.

Once, a frog was flattened by the meat
of a truck tire. He laid there for days

flat and lifeless as a shadow. His skin
scorched like the skin of a baked potato.

I checked on him every morning before school.
I wouldn't say that I admired or worshipped

his deadness, his color and sheen drained
from him, carried away or stitched into the dirt.

I just liked to know that he was still there,
some part of him, clinging to the earth.

Walking the Dog

The moon hangs
bright and low,
its iridescent glow
cast like dye
over our heads
as we walk together
stride for stride
in our shadows.
When we return
from the lake trail,
my face wrinkled
from the cold,
I feel as if we left
several years ago.

Your Body is a Galaxy

A perfect network of atoms
like the stars and planets
of the Milky Way. I watch
as you undress, in the few
moments we have alone,
without the kids. Before
you slip under the covers,
you stand for a few seconds
as naked, innocent and
beautiful as the day you
came into the world. In
these moments, I stare at you
as if through a telescope.
Your neck, so slender and
delicate, I sometimes wonder
how it manages to hold up
your head. Your eyes are deep
brown, wild stars. Your breasts,
snow-capped mountains. Only
warm and soft and round,
like cones built for milk and
pleasure. Your sternum is buried
in the crevasse between them.
Your nipples are as perfect as
nature intended. Areolas spread
across the soft skin of your breasts
like the rings of Saturn, their pigment
the perfect blend of chocolate.
The scar above your navel is
a reminder of your hernia, the
children you carried and bore.
The skin healing, folded in on itself
like the stitches dissolving underneath.
Your vagina tucked like a tulip between
the tender pages of my favorite book.
The soft white pages are your thighs.
There is a poem by Michael Dickman
called "Be More Beautiful"
and this is how it ends:
I wanted to be made out of nothing
but your voice / and be more beautiful /
and I was made. I've been trying
to think, for years, of one thing
that you could do to be more beautiful,
but I haven't come up with anything.

Stars & Trees

He'll be rambling on, no doubt,
About pigs and trees, stars and horses.
—Paul Muldoon, "Lunch with Pancho Villa"

The television static
of starlight
over the treeline
is just beyond our reach—
isn't it? I connect the dots,
mapping their contours
like the contours
of my wife's naked body
as she lies on her side
like Aphrodite.
We can't touch the sky,
but we can feel it, can't we?
The way we can feel heaven.
But we can't see heaven,
not in the way that we
can see the sky, at least.
I don't know if gods exist
or not. Perhaps I never will.
Perhaps I haven't looked
hard enough. But if my naked wife
lying in bed next to me is not a sign
that the goddess of beauty exists
then I don't know what is.

The Wise Old Oak

"Death steals everything except our stories"
—Jim Harrison, "Larson's Holstein Bull"

The stout trunk
of the barren oak
refuses to bend
in the wind.
It rarely speaks,
always listens.
Its watchful eye
has seen more life
than any man could live.
Before winter severed
the old oak's last limbs,
its wizened leaves
whispered stories
of countless seasons.
Trees die of thirst or cold
or when the limit's reached;
but death eludes this tree.
The closest thing on earth
to immortality
is the written word.
The wise old oak is waiting
for its story to be written.

Devils Tower

From a distance, the gnarled butte
looks more like tree than rock.

Two climbers scale its back,
their bodies stretched, rigid

and fragile as cold elastics—
two stars inching and inching

up the edges of its spine,
disappearing as the sun

brightens over the paved trail.
No one has spoken for a while.

The wind murmurs in the trees,
and I keep thinking about

the amount of time we spend
in miscommunication and silence.

Catfish

Wind hisses like snakes in the cordgrass.
We cross the wooden bridge over the marshland.
The streetlamps yellow glare filters through
cottonwood and pine, casting a pattern
of shadowy light upon the walking trail.
This summer, we passed a boy fishing here.
I asked him if he'd had any luck. His face lit up.
He opened his lunchbox and showed us two catfish
on a bed of half-melted ice. Grinning from ear to ear
like a hunter with a bull moose or ten-point buck,
packing his freezer for another long winter.

Crab Apple Tree

The window glass is
heavy with the scent
of my morning breath.
I'm watching deer graze
in the yellow light
on dewy grass
and fallen apples.
Worms consume
rot and excess
like maggots
on dead flesh.
Greedy ticks feed
on warm bodies.
Evening sets in—
the shadow of the
crab apple tree
stretches its arms
opens its mouth
and swallows the yard.

Giraffe

A giraffe eats lettuce from my son's hand.
Its tongue houses all the enthusiasm
its eyes lack. A blue-black snake —
thick, elongated. I am more impressed
by the prowess of the giraffe's tongue
than its neck or legs. Its tongue gets
no attention. It must be compressed
like a coil spring inside its mouth.
It turns out, the lump in my mother's
throat is likely benign, not malignant.
It expands and contracts like the giraffe's
tongue. After three consecutive biopsies,
the doctors know as much about her
condition, as I know about the giraffe.

Turkey Vulture

I listened to the brook
rolling over the rocks,
barely within earshot.

I watched the tall grass
dance in quiet fury.

A turkey vulture landed
on a bare patch of turf,
a small mound
just ahead.

It turned its ugly,
featherless head
in my direction—
its eyes wandering
on either side.

For a moment,
I thought the world
might be more beautiful
without it.

I held my finger over the trigger
of my older brother's pellet gun
and I thought long and hard
about pulling it.

The Bear

The water danced like ribbon
over the jagged rocks
as they made their way
across the brook.
Dense woodland was all that stood
between them and their camp.
They stepped around
the bear tracks in the trail
as they made their way uphill.
The snap and crunch
of twig and brush
hushed their voices
as they stepped out
into a small clearing.
The forest was so quiet
they could hear their breath
and feel their hearts
beating like fists in their chests
when the bear lifted its head
and stared in their direction.
They backed away slowly
keeping the bear visible
on the periphery.
When he stepped toward them
they took off like two birds
startled from a branch.
They weaved through the trees
never looking back
or checking in
until they reached the brook.
When they looked back
to where they came from
the bear was gone.
They were left by the brook
with nothing more or less
than their heavy breath
and a story to tell.
They had entered

the house of the bear
and lived to tell the tale.
There was no going back.
The camp belonged
to the woods now.
I swear my friends told me
this is how it happened
even though it was nearly
twenty years ago now.
I wasn't there, so I can't say.
But I think the bear took flight
like a frightened bird
faster than they could
when he heard their voices
and the fallen branches
snapping beneath their feet.
The two of them and the bear
ran as fast as their legs
would carry them
in different directions.

Westfield

The sun beat down
like golden wings
over a sea of birch
and apple trees.
We were only boys,
but we felt the breeze
of autumn on our
sun-ripened skin
as if we were small gods.

Small Gods

The god of weather
spits snow sideways
through yellow teeth.
A modern-day Odin,
his weathered face
wrinkled, broken in
as a leather saddle
on a stubborn horse.
Not to mention
his one good eye
the other made of glass,
his pupil and iris scrambled
in their socket like albumen
and yolk in a bowl,
or his infinite wisdom.
Jim Harrison's words
remind me constantly
how as a child I roamed
freely through the woods
and now I am tethered
like a leaf to a tree
to my responsibilities.
Someday, I'll go back
and visit the distant places
of my past. Someday,
I'll go back. I wonder
if the gods of my youth
still exist. I'm trying
not to lose faith.

The Chapel

In the quiet hours
wind howls
and snow drifts
like mountains.

The fire burning
in the hearth
of the chapel,
in the heart
of birch and frost
is not lost
on this wilderness.

These are the keys
to our survival
and comfort—
necessary fragments
of our domestic,
modern world:

knife, tent, firestarter,
pen and paper, a good book
and a sack lunch—
companions we carry with us
like torches into the wild.

The Wild

I believe the great beauty
of the natural world
hides in the uninhabitable:
rivers and lakes without camp
or cottage, overgrown hedges,
wild ferns, birch and cypress,
mountains of rock and moss.
I remember stepping out
from a tunnel of trees
off the crooked trail
in the Cloud Peak Wilderness.
Looking out over a glistening lake
that rested like a hammock
below the tree and skyline.
There was nothing but
water, tree and mountain
for miles. Along the shore
all the trees had fallen—
trunks and limbs entangled,
woven together like mesh
armor to protect the water,
lake grass and fish from debris
and litter. Nothing could enter
without dipping under
or climbing over the border
nature had built for itself.
The fish jumped,
splashed and kicked as if
they had never been prey
to anything but time.
A man stood on a rock
reeling in and casting his line
endlessly into the lake.
This place could not occur naturally.
Time could never build this.
This place was sculpted
by the hands of gods.
Created for us as a haven

Bodies

of peace, treaties and worship.
I believe in the voices of birds,
the woodpecker hammering away
at the tree, and the bull moose
dipping its head toward the lake
to slake its thirst. We desperately
wanted to come across something—
anything living, to feel more alive.
But the blood coursing through
our veins, the altitude we reached
and the sights we managed to see
were enough. There is beauty
everywhere if you know where
to look. We seek out these moments
of intimate, personal beauty
and the words to describe them.
If we knew where to find either,
that is exactly where we'd look.
The great beauty of the natural world
hides in the uninhabitable—
it can't be tamed. It's wild and free.
I believe in tragedy and love
and heartbreak. And I believe
that this is a place the soul needs
to rest and feel at peace.
I believe that if the soul could speak
it would use its final words
to describe such a place.

Acknowledgements and Notes

Grateful acknowledgments are due to the editors of the following publications where some of these poems, or earlier versions of them, were published:

Red Eft Review: "The Chapel"

Eunoia Review: "Mountains," "Giraffe"

34 Orchard: "The Doe"

Dreich: "Mosquitoes", "Discovery", "Skinning a Deer", "Turkey Vulture," "Soul Birds," "The Bear"

Black Cat Poetry Press: "Mother"

Vita Brevis: "Anxiety"

Voices de la Luna: "San Antonio"

Soor Ploom Press: "Horse", "Rabbit"

"The Middle of the Night" and "Bodies" are anthologized in *Hope Is A Group Project*, published by The Wee Sparrow Poetry Press.

"Spring" was inspired by the opening line of Shangyang Fang's poem, "Tether" and the sporadic Wyoming weather.

"Peacock" was inspired by the Nanga paintings of Taika Okahara.

"Trying on Tuxedos" was inspired by my brother and sister-in-law's wedding, and Ellen Bass's poem "The Orange-and-White High-Heeled Shoes."

"The Chapel" was inspired by a winter landscape painting by Ryan Owens.

The phrase "bass chorus" is from Seamus Heaney's poem, "Death of a Naturalist."

The lines, "Trees die of thirst or cold / or when the limit's reached" are from Jim Harrison's poem "John Severin Walgren, 1874-1962."

Gratitude to the Wyoming Arts Council and the private donor who makes the Neltje Blanchan Memorial Writing Award possible.

Thank you to Nicholas Trandahl for your invaluable insight, and for being a tremendous friend, mentor and first reader. Deep gratitude to my teachers and professors, for fostering my love of literature and poetry. Thank you to Camille Dungy, for transforming these poems at the last minute. Thank you to Jim Harrison, Ted Kooser, Dan Gerber, Raymond Carver, Mary Oliver, Shangyang Fang, Ellen Bass, Ada Limón, Seamus Heaney and Paul Muldoon for writing the kind of poems that I need to read and aspire to write. Thank you to my editor, Ryan Collins, for your trust in me and your faith in this manuscript. Thank you to my parents, for your encouragement and support. Finally, thank you Jacqlyn McQuade, my wife and muse, for your enduring love and inspiration, and for affording me the time and freedom to pursue this dream.